PRINCIPAL WORKS OF ALBERTO SAVINIO

FICTION

Hermaphrodito, 1918; *La casa ispirata*, 1925
Angelica o la notte di maggio, 1927
Tragedia dell'infanzia, 1937; *Achille innamorato*, 1938
Infanzia di Nivasio Dolcemare, 1941
Dico a te, Clio, 1941
Ascolto il tuo cuore, città, 1943
Casa "La Vita", 1943; *La nostra anima*, 1944
Tutta la vita, 1945; *L'angolino*, 1950

ESSAYS

Seconda vita di Gemito, 1938; *Leo Longanesi*, 1942
Narrate, uomini, la vostra storia, 1942
Scatola sonora, 1955; *Maupassant e "l'altro"*, 1960

PLAYS

Capitan Ulisse, 1929; *La famiglia Mastinu*, 1948
Emma B. vedova Giocasta, 1949
Alcesti di Samuele, 1949; *Orfeo vedovo*, 1950

Speaking to Clio

Alberto Savinio

Speaking to Clio

Translated by John Shepley

THE MARLBORO PRESS
MARLBORO, VERMONT
1987

Originally published in Italian as
DICO A TE, CLIO
Copyright © 1946 G. C. Sansoni, Florence

Manufactured in the United States of America

Library of Congress Catalog Card Number 86-63743

Cloth: ISBN 0-910395-22-5
Paper: ISBN 0-910395-23-3

THE MARLBORO PRESS

MARLBORO, VERMONT

AUTHOR'S NOTE

Of the two books now being reissued by the publisher, Sansoni (*Tragedia dell'infanzia* [*Tragedy of Childhood*] is from 1920, *Speaking to Clio* from 1939), the first is a forest, the second a garden. *Tragedia dell'infanzia* is a forest for the darkness that grows thicker in that most murky season of life; *Speaking to Clio* is a garden for the clarity, lightness, and amenity that I acquired in my mature years.

From that story to these journeys, the astute reader will above all be able to measure the passage from a raw dish to a cooked one.

For in *bonae litterae* as well as in cuisine, it's all a matter of cooking.

A. S. (Rome, 1946)

Speaking to Clio

Clio: χλείω: I close. *History collects our actions and gradually deposits them in the past. History gradually frees us from the past. A perfect organization of life would ensure that all our actions, even the least and most insignificant, become history, so as to relieve us of them, take them off our backs. The habit of consigning our daily actions to a diary is a rule of hygiene, and the man with an active mind is implicitly a memorialist, who deposits his "inner actions" in his memoirs, that is to say in his works. We ought to get in the habit as children of keeping a diary, just as we get in the habit of brushing our teeth. As for washing our face in the morning, we do it to cleanse it of our dreams, those "actions" of sleep, those nocturnal "sins." That civilization will be perfect that translates everything into history and allows us to rediscover ourselves each morning in a fresh condition, free from the past. What we obtain by history, others obtain by confession, and we call actions what they call sins. Using the same language, we can say that any action is sin, and living, this uninter- rupted sequence of actions, is a continual process of sinning. Some also put poetry among the forms of catharsis, saying that poetry frees us from the slavery of passion, but they are wrong. Poetry — and the arts, instruments of poetry — has no relations with passion, but makes use of incorruptible elements that lie beyond passion. Of course, I am here speaking of poetry in its metaphysical quality. The ills of the world, its slowness, its obstacles, its stupidity, can be attributed to the incomplete functioning of history. The past festers on some men and*

1

rots. *In the proper darkness, they would shine from the filth coating them like a crust. Heaps of "unhistorified" material choke the pathways of the world. This constant throwing of the past over one's shoulder, this constant "self-purification" . . . So does life have an end? In the last gaze coming from our eyes, the last light from our intelligence, that gaze, that light, will not be directed to the past, placed for good behind the closed door, but to the future. And the future, as you will have understood, ladies and gentlemen, is death, inaction par excellence and supreme purity.*

The malfunctioning of history is compensated in part by an unwritten history, a non-oral history, a non-mnemonic history, a history "nonhistorical" but a natural and spontaneous catharsis: a "ghost" of history. The absurd axiom, the cruel axiom, the forced axiom that "nothing is lost in nature" has finally been belied. Beyond the murkiest depths, beyond the most unfathomable abysses, our souls will recognize the true goal of life: to disappear. Alongside history, which gradually stops the actions of men, confines them, and makes them inoperative, there is the ghost of history: the great hole, the void that little by little absorbs the actions that escape history and annihilates them. Our extraordinary sight, made extraordinarily acute in an extraordinary moment of our lives, has allowed us for a moment to see once again the annihilated actions inside that void, the deeds that no longer exist, the vanished vicissitudes, the things that no one will ever be able to see again. A very thin garden, in which the ghosts of the flowers were dying. And if the annihilated deeds were the only memorable ones? What if the greatest destiny of human vicissitudes, the noblest, highest, "holiest" fate of ourselves and our thoughts were not history, but the ghost of history?

Arnold Böcklin used to prepare his canvases in gray; then with a sponge soaked in water he would lay out in large masses the composition he had in mind; finally he would sit down and contemplate for a long time this preliminary ghost of his new work. If the damp sketch satisfied him, he would go back over it with paint and fix its outlines; if not, he allowed it little by little to fade away.

Works that enter into history — works that enter into the ghost of history.

Memories, too, slowly but inexorably fade.

That morning Charun, he who escorts souls from this life to the other, awakened me and told me it was time to go. I didn't even think of asking to see his arrest warrant, and followed him without saying a word.

Ari, 12 August 1939

On our host's terrace, at Ari. His name sounds strange outside Abruzzo: it is Concezio. We are in the situation of a painting by Hans von Thoma, the last of the German Romantic painters. In this artist's panoramic landscapes, a figure placed in the foreground looks at the landscape with obvious satisfaction, as though inviting the spectator to do likewise. At Ari, the role of the "decoy" figure is played in the flesh by Concezio. With his finger he traces a slow semicircle over the panorama and says, "Here we are in the Chietino." At the unexpected resonance of this geographical designation, we look at each other in the fear of having misunderstood.

Concezio weighs well over two hundred pounds and is proportionately tall. Other times we had been saddened by the thought that the race of giants had disappeared, but Concezio has brought joy back to our hearts. The day before yesterday, on the beach at the Pineta di Pescara, we saw him in a bathing suit: two tufts of tawny hair sprout like small oases in the middle of the powerful desert of his shoulders. He wanted to take the wheel of our Topolino in order to try it out, but the poor "compact" sagged on its left wheel and refused to move. The Abruzzese abhors the small. He says that from the *sfetature* of the hen, meaning the eggs as small as pigeon eggs, the basilisk serpent is born, that is to say the devil. Basilisk is also what he calls the undersized fetus produced by a woman, who in this case has not given birth to a child, but *ha fatte 'nu bascialische.* A legend cited by Athenaeus gives the origin of this superstition and the explanation of the word "basilisk." A king of the Spartans had taken as his wife a woman of short stature, while his subjects complained that in this way they were planning not to produce a king but a kinglet: *non rex sed regulus,* and in Greek *basiliscos.*

At the edge of the Pineta di Pescara is a sign: "Pineta Dannunziana." I am not blinded by love for the poetry of d'Annunzio. I pride myself on being one of the very few Italians completely immune to d'Annunzianism. Besides I was absent from Italy at the time of the great d'Annunzian fervor, and it may be for this reason that things concerning d'Annunzio now strike me as so new. I gaze with curiosity on the little forest, which I know to have been his "inspiration." It upholds with elegance the tall trunks of its pinè trees, ostriches of the vegetable kingdom. In response to my wonder, the pine grove frees itself from its arboreal nature and takes on the shape of a woman. Thus is anthropomorphism born.

Sadness, the great burden of giants, is lacking in Concezio. Grave affliction darkens the brow of the Farnese Hercules, and bends his body over his cudgel. "The sculptor," writes Schlegel, "has depicted the son of Alcmene after one of his famous labors." As though before the labor the son of Alcmene had been a jolly fellow. The rule conceals the truth, and the exceptions are so many "whys" scattered here and there like marking stakes. Concezio is an exception, an amiable monster, a kobold's soul in the body of Gyges. *Mens agitat molem.* The house where we are staying was not always used for habitation. Concezio's grandfather took part in the parliamentary life of the first legislatures, and had given this house a political function. During the electoral campaign he would gather the sixty or seventy voters who constituted the majority in the municipality and keep them shut up in this house until election day, wining and dining them unstintingly. "My grandfather," concludes Concezio, "was never defeated." And how could he have been, if he treated those lucky prisoners to the same wine that today glistens on the table in our honor, and has been pressed from these vines that run in ordered, verdant rows down the slope on which our host's little house stands and climb the slope of the opposite hill across the valley? It is the whitest wine imaginable, the albino of wines, and terribly deceptive. The glass, when full, looks empty; but what soul in this wine transparent as the breath of a newborn baby, what fire! Johannisberg or Chablis do not stand up by comparison.

While we drink to Bacchus Lyaeus (Bacchus who loosens: so much truth in this word!), the parent bunches hang plump from the pergola over our heads, swept by fumes and illusions.

A curious village! Heavy and very light at the same time, northern and at the same time Greek. Around it a solidified tempest of mountains and valleys. At the top of each "wave" sits a little village with the hump of its large church and the upraised finger of its bell tower. These little villages have been built stone by stone by dark, patient little men who gradually emerged from the valleys, but their lofty position, their nestlike appearance suggest rather that they were built from above by those bird men whom Cyrano de Bergerac met on his extraordinary travels. Cyrano was a light poet, with an unraveled imagination, and how different, how much better than the verbose clown that Rostand filled with hot air and alexandrines and a few old windbags still tote around on our stages like a model of poetry. Rostand was of that dangerous species that spoils everything it touches. Cyrano's tirades have echoed in our military life, from the latrines in the barracks. What fascination does this poetry have for the soldier at the moment of relieving himself?

One of the little villages that can be seen from our host's pergola is called Turi. A great melancholy used to descend from time to time on the Turians. One by one they would go outside the village, scatter themselves among the vineyards or in the shadows of the olive trees, aim their double-barreled shotguns under their chins, and blow off their heads like corks from a bottle of spumante. All the men in these parts are hunters.

Another of these rocky little villages, which you can see from the road leading to Francavilla, is Migliànico. Its church is even larger and more humped than the others, and its bell tower more "didactic." It was in the church of Migliànico that Francesco Paolo Michetti saw the scene that inspired him to paint *Il voto* (The Vow). The figures in this famous painting are posed in creeping motions; the peasant in the foreground, prone on the floor of the church and resting on the tips of his fingers, is executing one of the better known Müller gymnastic exercises. These figures are not performing an act of devotion as one might have thought, but practicing a ritualistic rubbing cure. Phenomena of religious mass psychosis are quite frequent in these parts, but Michetti himself may not have been aware of the real reason for these positions. In Sulmona, up until a few years ago, those afflicted with stomachache used to go and sit on *Saint Pamphilus' chair*. Those suffering from rheumatism go and rub the ailing part on the walls of the church. More curious is the fact that in Ari (the village where we find ourselves) those with lumbago go and rub their backs not on the holy walls of the church, but on the wall of the town hall, or else on a rural boundary stone. Simultaneously they repeat three times:

> *Tèrmene, che sti piandàte,*
> *Famm'aresajje' 'sti lumme che mme se n'è ccalàte.*

> (Stone, well planted in the earth,
> Lift up these fallen loins of mine.)

We have taken the information on these rubbing rituals from *Miti, leggende e superstizioni dell'Abruzzo* by Giovanni Pansa (vol. I, chap. 5), and by a happy coincidence it is the very granddaughter of this illustrious scholar from Sulmona who is giving us such gracious hospitality in her pleasant country house.

There are valid reasons to support the idea of the bird origins of these rocky little villages. Bird men abound in these parts, and a very common surname in Abruzzo is Celidonio, which surely comes from *chelidon*, swallow. What a pity! The cutting flight of this bird of spring (in spring itself there is something disagreeable), its shrill and vexing cry, are disturbing and a reminder that madness lies waiting. *Est in arundinis modulatio musica ripis.* The myth of the three swallow sisters is significant. Athena had entrusted to Aglauros, Herse, and Pandrosos a basket in which she had hidden Erichthonius, with the express command not to open it. But the three sisters could not resist their curiosity, whereupon they were set upon by the Furies and threw themselves over a cliff, being transformed at that same instant into swallows. Beware of the swallow! If she could speak, the "little nun" would invite us to suicide. And to think that the swallow passes for a "bearer of good tidings," while the poor bat, which if nothing else is a mammal like you and me and sucks its mother's milk, is so despised and feared!

At dinner, the day before yesterday, the courses followed each other as numerous and copious as ever, but without meat. Then I remembered it was Friday. In Abruzzo, prime considerations are more alive than elsewhere, the stony gaze more felt of those Mothers whom Faust descended into the bowels of the earth to interrogate. What power has the mountain over man's religious mind? These mountain walls transform the village into a natural temple, and geography has placed the man of Abruzzo in the favored place of prayer and faith. Here the expectation of a miracle is a living hope, as is for us the expectation of love, happiness, or fame. Abruzzo is a vast crèche that moves to the sound of bagpipes.

Ari, 14 August

Yesterday morning, Sunday, while driving down to Francavilla, we met an old woman who was walking along the dusty road, wearing, like a black monument, the heavy accumulation of her holiday clothes. It was Assunta, a peasant who works for our hosts. Every Sunday at dawn she sets out from Ari and walks the thirty kilometers separating it from Pescara, in order to pay her respects to her son, an apprentice in a machine shop. She takes him two eggs and a little fresh cheese; then slowly she returns, dragging her tower of dark clothes in the dust, and in the middle of the night she is back in Ari.

Instead of praising this maternal devotion, I ask why the mother goes down to visit the son rather than the son going up to visit the mother.

The past is eager for adventures, but without reciprocity. That young apprentice probably feels that by returning from the city to the village, he would betray that destiny which, like the locomotive, has eyes only for looking in front of itself. Legend (Lot's wife) joins with philosophy (Weininger) in exhorting man not to turn around.

15

We stop at a spring to drink. Women and children are standing around in Anacreontic poses, basins resting on one hip. Every spring is a dispenser of life: this one moreover dispenses miracles. But it doesn't show it, and even those who are miraculously cured remain in ignorance. We are told that neither Fiuggi water, nor Tettuccio, nor Chianciano can equal the virtues of this water, which flows freely and generously for everybody. But why waste a diuretic and cathartic water to wash salad and rinse clothes? The owner of this spring has been converted to Buddhism and spends many hours of the day kneeling before a blank wall, as though before an invisible altar. The race of Schopenhauers is not yet extinct, and Buddha teaches one to be lavish with good. We too took a long drink from the miraculous spring, but with no effect. Are we therefore unreceptive to miracles?

Guardiagrele, 15 August

We left early for Guardiagrele. The name of this city has a military ring to it. D'Annunzio calls it "city of stone," which is like saying nothing. Unless you're referring to Russian cities prior to the reign of Ivan III, the word "city" naturally evokes the idea of stone. The historian of Guardiagrele lived in the sixth century, but his name was like that of any of us: Pasquale Carlini. Pasquale Carlini's manuscript was preserved by the Benedictines of San Clemente a Comino. "Grele," says Pasquale Carlini, "was situated on what was almost a plain, east of the Majella. It was destroyed by a severe earthquake in the year A.D. 83. It had existed for 1200 years before the Christian era and was named for a temple that stood on the site where today stands the church of the Virgin Mary, a temple dedicated to the Sun, that is, to Apollo, also called Helios. Temples built to Jove, Janus, and Diana remain and are used today for Christian worship. The Samnites called it Aelion, the Greeks Graelio, from the name of their leader, the Romans Grelium, whence Greli, and the barbarians Graele, Graelle, Grela, and later Guardia di Graelle, Guardiagrele."

17

No greater suffering . . . You must travel by these secondary roads, where even today your vehicle is followed by a twisting plume of dust like the tail of a comet, to understand the great virtue of paved roads. We go through Filetto and Orsogna. Despite its name, we do not find in Filetto so much as a *filetto di benzina,* a trickle of gasoline, and not even a pharmacy retailing this precious liquid. What do the inhabitants of Filetto use for spot-remover?

The name of Orsogna sounds as though it were invented by Gabriele d'Annunzio. They say that when the news reached Orsogna of its first soldier killed in war, the voice not only of his mother but of all the mothers of Orsogna was raised in the night and crackled until dawn, like the flame of a vast conflagration. The natural scenery of tragedy that surrounds this village also rouses the characters of tragedy, and their voices. Aeschylus is more Abruzzese than Eleusian.

Guardiagrele appears to the motorist like New York to the navigator. This reduction does not bother anyone who knows how to look at things with Greek eyes, that is, to see the large in the small. In order to paint his dragons, Böcklin took as his model those little fish that we eat head, tail, and all, and which are called smelts. This "insular" city is girdled with skyscrapers. Minuscule skyscrapers, of two or three stories at the most, but skyscrapers all the same for the proportion between width and height. Let me add that the skyscrapers of Guardiagrele are not the product of rhetoric and ambition, like those of San Babila in Milan or Piazza Castello in Turin, but of specific reasons of space. Like that of

Manhattan, the area of Guardiagrele is also enclosed within strict limits.

At this point our journey becomes sonorous. The sight of the skyscrapers awakens a vein of melody in Concezio. The automobile is filled with a Guardiagrele song, a mountaineers' tune. Concezio and the two *citeli* sing the melody, and the Signora Mariangela does the counterpoint. In Abruzzo children are called *citeli* or *quadrali*. The song is as solemn and melancholy as befits an Abruzzese song, but how can you follow its languid inflections when Concezio starts driving with his left hand and beating time with his right, while the automobile careens fearfully on the brink of ravines and precipices?

Cement is the "vulgarity" of our time. Alongside the most ordinary stone, the block of cement is like a wax nose stuck on a face of flesh. In addition to soul, cement lacks inwardness. It is as empty and dismal as a dead thing. Compare the ignobleness of damaged cement with the touching nobility of damaged marble. It is hard to understand why in a quarry of beautiful and living stones such as Italy they should build with cement, but there is a reason, and it is not facility but a certain kind of art. The *ideal* of the bad sculptor is to represent, by means of the materials of which statuary makes use, that which by its nature is quite different from the hardness and inflexibility of these materials, i.e., the soft, the supple, the delicate. Compare this "ideal" with the "ideal" of the bad poet to *express the inexpressible*. Bernini cut marble as though it were Provolone cheese, but Art Nouveau found in cement the way to surpass even

Cavalier Bernini, and the aspiration to give full flight to draperies, full quiver to foliage, and full swell to waves was achieved.

The public gardens of Guardiagrele have duly been called "the balcony of Abruzzo," because they overlook, if not really all, a great many of the Abruzzese mountains and valleys. Near the terrace slumbers an artificial pond, spanned by a cement bridge. The balustrade of the bridge is of cement and imitates interwoven tree trunks.

Under the garden trees, our gaze meets the nocturnal gaze, laden with unfulfillable dreams, of a dark-haired young woman. She is sprawled rather than seated on a bench, next to an elderly gentleman, with straw hat and pince-nez, who is quietly reading a newspaper. And we had thought that Emma Bovary was dead . . .

There is also an artificial pond in the public gardens of Ortona, and the cement bridge spanning it also has a balustrade made in imitation of interwoven tree trunks. Ortona is a splendid little city and its high promenade above the sea is worthy of a wounded and sorrowing Tristan. But also in Ortona there is the monument to Francesco Paolo Tosti. The "Master of Melody" (I transcribe the inscription on the monument) is shown bearded and with bags under his eyes in the form of a squeezed and very narrow bust, above a troop of maidens in nightgowns who sing and hold hands. I recommend as a detail of the modeling the folds of the nightgowns. Onatas the sculptor, before setting his hand to his famous statue of Hera, summoned the goddess to visit him in a dream and instruct him how she wanted to